Contents

Menacing Monsters: The Facts   5

Not Friendly!   25

4

THUNDER BOLTS

Menacing Monsters

by
David Orme

Ransom

Thunderbolts

Menacing Monsters
by David Orme

Illustrated by Leon Active

Published by Ransom Publishing Ltd.
Radley House, 8 St. Cross Road, Winchester, Hants. SO23 9HX, UK
www.ransom.co.uk

ISBN   978 178127 064 6
First published in 2013

Copyright © 2013 Ransom Publishing Ltd.

Illustrations copyright © 2013 Leon Active
'Get the Facts' section - images copyright: cover, prelims, passim – Bob Kupbens, Blueag9, Jan Benda; pp 4/5 - André Karwath aka Aka; pp 6/7 - Bob Kupbens, Alexander Omelko, JanRehschuh, Mats Stafseng Einarsen; pp 8/9 - Alexander Omelko, Peter_Nile, Hans Hillewaert; pp 10/11 - Allan Tooley, Andrew Howe, J.M. Luijt; pp 12/13 - FunkMonk (Michael B. H.), Wallace63, Tracy O, Sabrina Pintus; pp 14/15 - Ronnie Sampson, Hsing-Wen Hsu, Matt Craven, Matthias Hutter; pp 16/17 - Timur Kulgarin, Marie-Lan Nguyen, Findlay Rankin, bülent gültek; pp 18/19 - Citron; pp 20/21 - Marilyn Nieves, Sergey Mironov; pp 22/23 - Natalia Lukiyanova; p 36 - Blueag9.

A CIP catalogue record of this book is available from the British Library.

All rights reserved. No part of this publication may be reproduced, stored in a retrieval system, or transmitted, in any form or by any means, electronic, mechanical, photocopying, recording or otherwise, without the prior permission of the publishers.

The rights of David Orme to be identified as the author and of Leon Active to be identified as the illustrator of this Work have been asserted by them in accordance with sections 77 and 78 of the Copyright, Design and Patents Act 1988.

Menacing Monsters: The Facts

Monster animals

Anaconda

Komodo dragon

Gila monster

Aargh! What's this?

Find out on the next page.

More monster animals

Great white shark

Common squid

What is this?
It's a stag beetle.

Meat-eating dinosaurs

Velociraptor

A Tarbosaurus

Tyrannosaurus rex

11

After the dinosaurs

Sabre-tooth cat

12

Woolly mammoth

'Terror bird'

Are they real?

This is Loch Ness. Is that a monster?

Dragons

Yeti. Are they real?

15

Monsters from myths

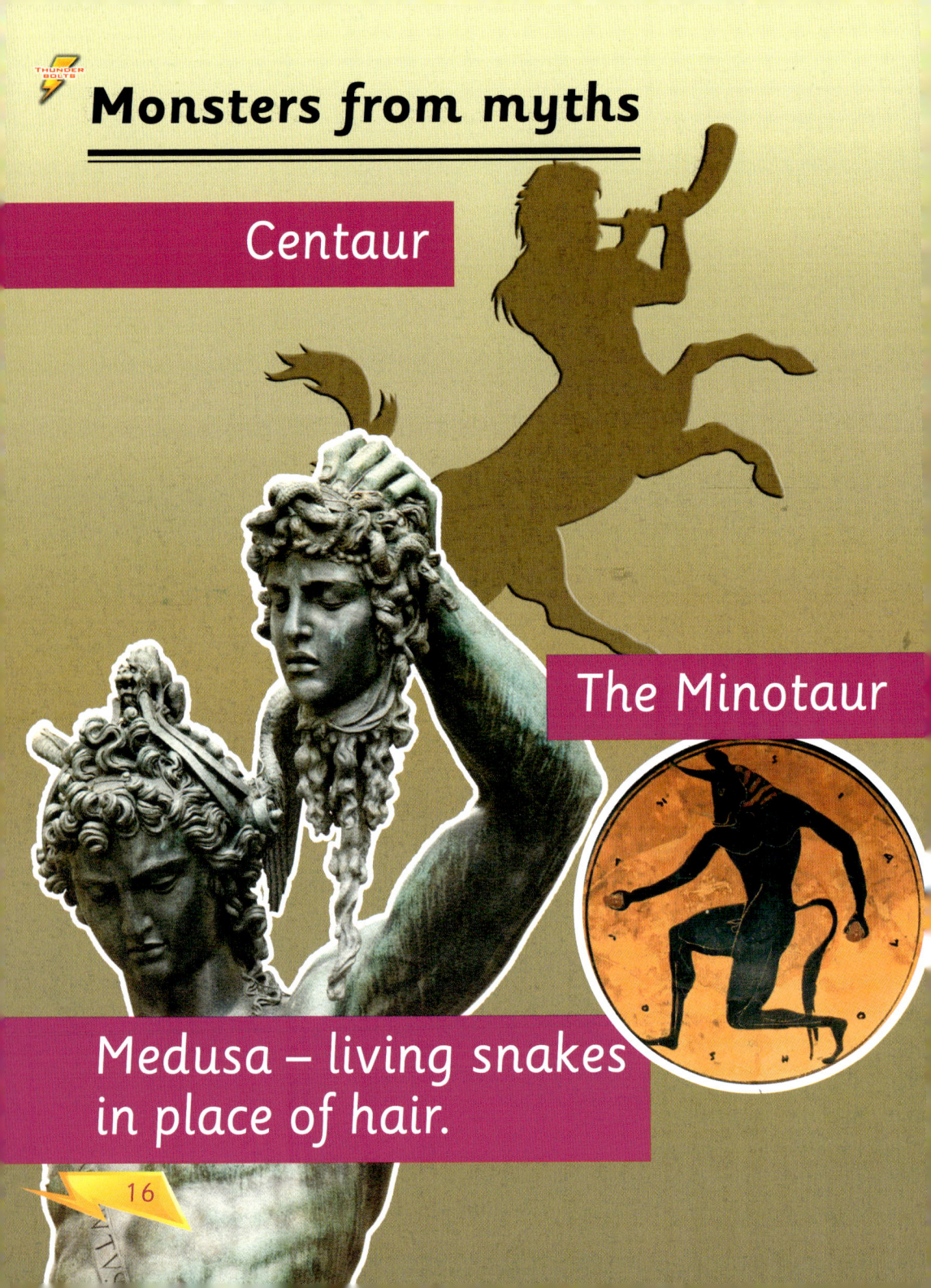

Centaur

The Minotaur

Medusa – living snakes in place of hair.

Cyclops

17

The kraken

The kraken was a huge sea monster.

Was it real?

18

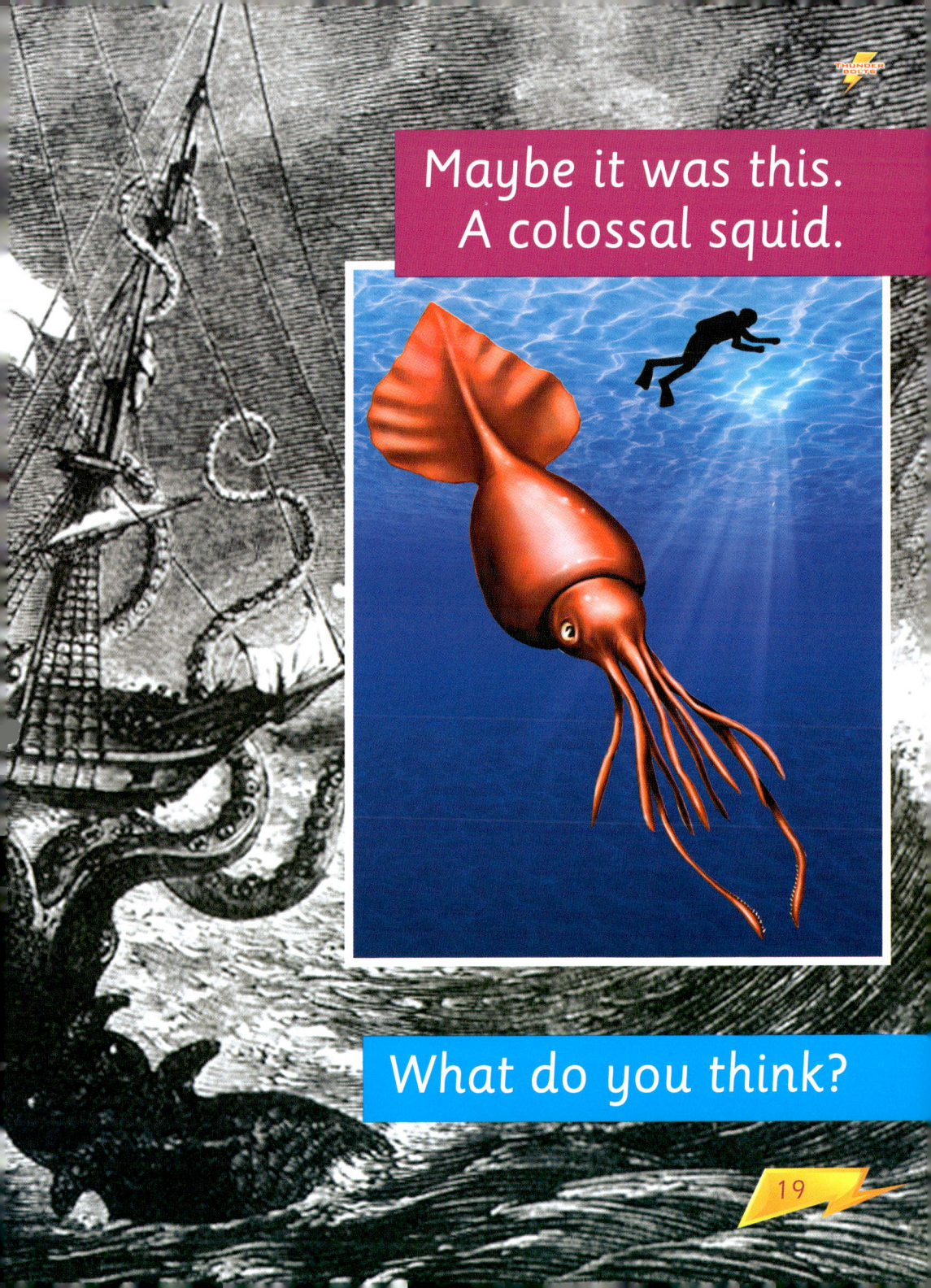

Maybe it was this.
A colossal squid.

What do you think?

19

Werewolves and vampires

When it's a full moon, some people turn into werewolves!

Really?

Er ... no.

Vampires love blood.

21

Aliens. Will they be friendly?

I don't think so!

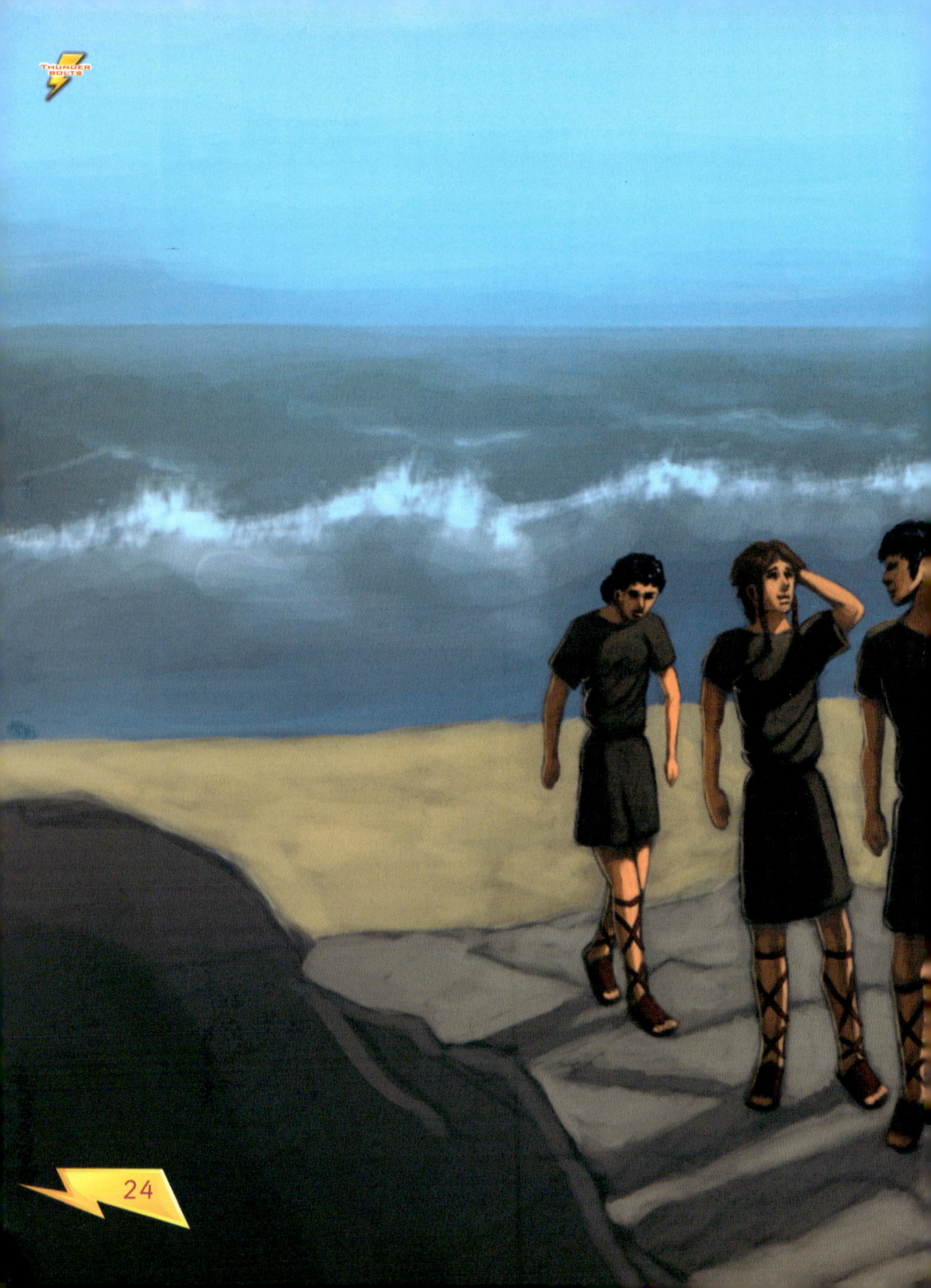

Not Friendly!

These sailors have got lost ...

"An island!"

Not friendly!

27

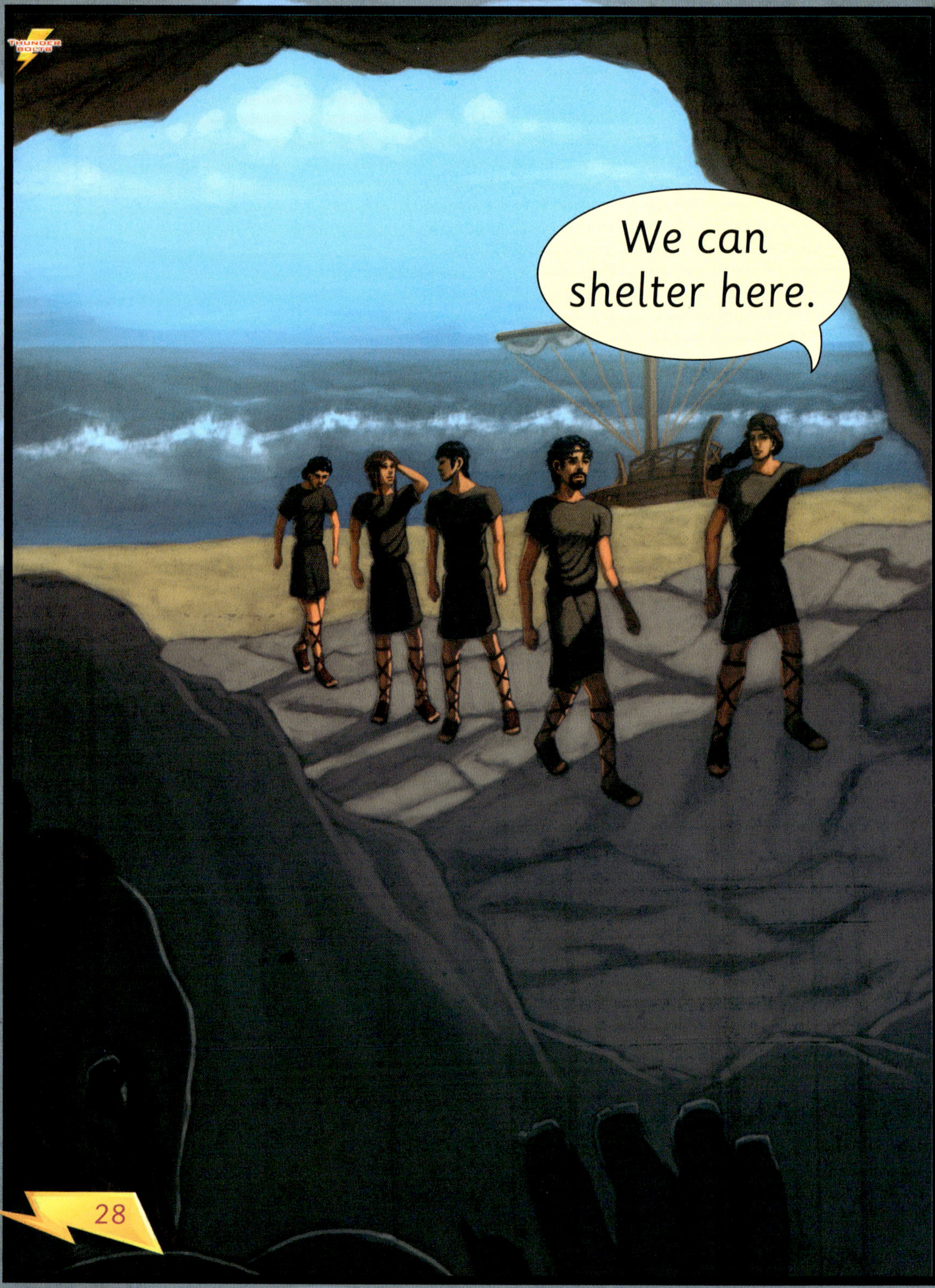
We can shelter here.

Then ...

Ah! Dinner!

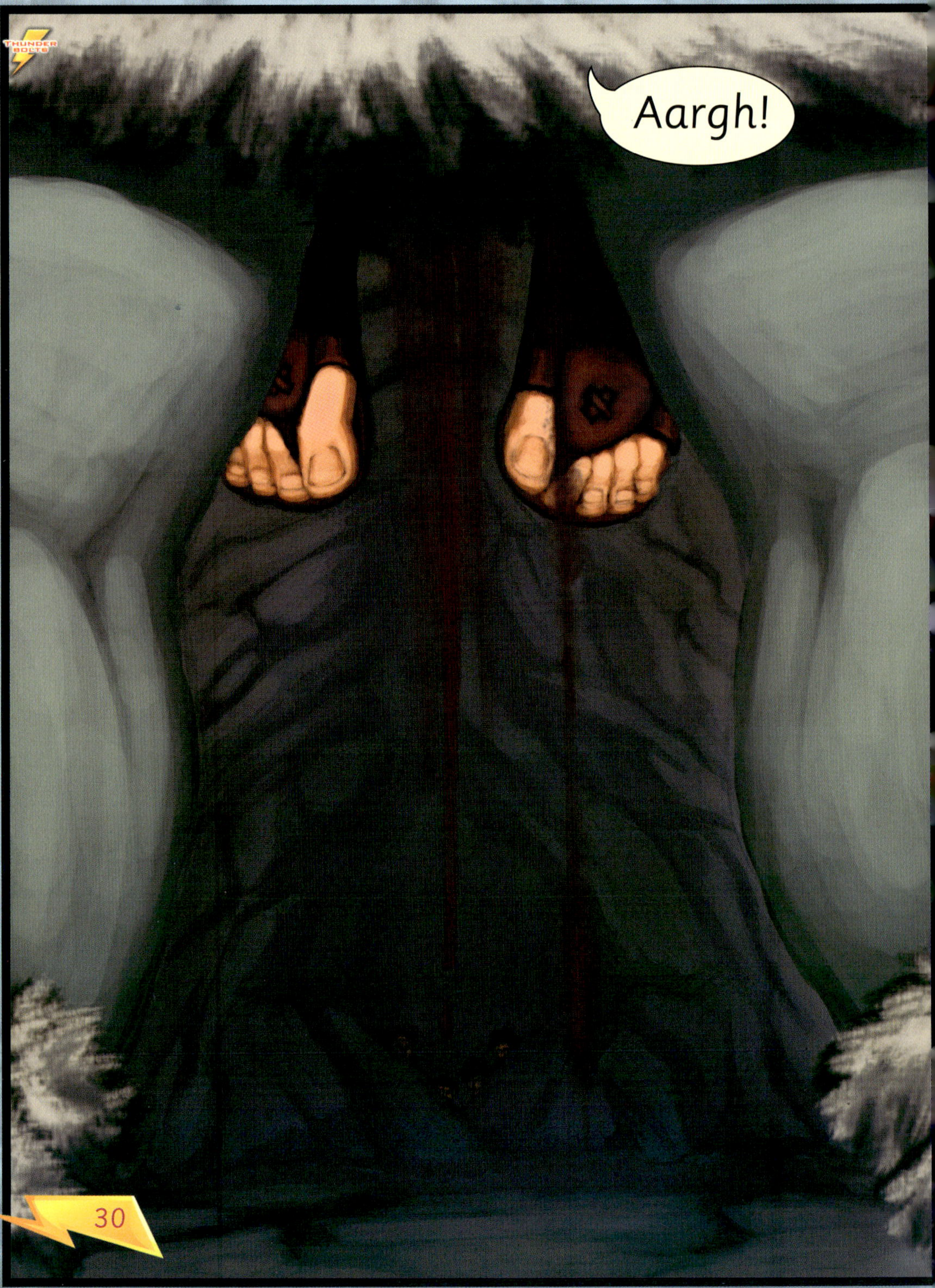
Aargh!

Later …

I've got an idea!

"Let's go for it!"

"I can't see!!"

But ...

I've got a plan!

So ...

34

Word list

alien
anaconda
centaur
colossal squid
common squid
cyclops
dragon
Gila monster
great white shark
komodo dragon
kraken
Loch Ness
Medusa

Minotaur
monster
sabre-tooth cat
stag beetle
Tarbosaurus
terror bird
Tyrannosaurus rex
vampire
Velociraptor
werewolf
woolly mammoth
Yeti